Psalms Journal

Psalms Journal

A 21-Day Devotional Journal

Psalms Journal is a devotional workbook inviting you to reflect and journal on 21 selected Psalms, examining what they say about God and how they connect to your life; all while forming (or enhancing) a habit of journaling and prayer.

CONTRIBUTORS:

HENRY MIERSMA

TIM SPYKSTRA

DAVID TANIS, D. ED

MILL STREET PRESS

SAN LUIS OBISPO, CA

Psalms Journal

Published by Mill Street Press

P.O. Box 432

San Luis Obispo, CA 93406

ISBN 978-0-9990722-2-6

TABLE OF CONTENTS

THE 21-DAY JOURNALING CHALLENGE

Foreword

Discovering God's Heart in The Psalms

Ahead of you is an amazing journey, one which will open up spiritual vistas with life-transforming implications. I'm both excited and thankful for my good friend Henry who has answered God's call to put this vitally needed tool together for such a time as this.

We are living in a time when so many broken souls need encouragement—both believers in the battle and also those searching for truth amid a fuzzy, uncertain culture. I believe the Psalms provide that encouragement.

For centuries, the Psalms have cried out to weary and lonely travelers to come and find a home overflowing with a wrap-around love that will never let go. I can testify to this blessed gift as for years I have begun each day walking through the Psalms into my Father's gracious presence. This rhythm has challenged, convicted, corrected, comforted, and carried me through countless storms in life.

In this workbook you will practice disciplines that will help you open the door to deeper experiences of true belonging. The combination of reading and listening to the Word, journaling thoughts and truths, and wrapping them together with praise and prayer will awaken you to the Father's grace-filled heart toward you.

I am certain that if you embark on this journey for twenty-one days, dwelling in these selected psalms, you will find a path into His presence that will touch the deepest need of your thirsty soul. You will encounter a loving Father, His saving Son, and the gift of the Holy Spirit dwelling in your heart.

I praise God in advance for all the blessed fruit that will abound to those who take the steps of faith into these psalms through this journal. All our world desperately needs can be discovered in the pages that follow.

– Tim Spykstra

Preface

How's Your Walk with God?

My good friend Doug calls me on a regular basis to ask how I'm doing. When I answer the phone, the first thing he says is, "Hey, Henry, how's your walk with God?" Every time! We'll cover a lot of subjects during the call, but first we chat about *our walk*.

To me, walking with God is about our call as believers to live according to God's Word and prioritize our relationship with Him. I believe *walking* implies a level of intimacy that results from regularly slowing down and spending extended time alone with Him.

So whenever I hear Doug's question, I interpret it as his way of asking, "Are you spending an appropriate amount of your time studying God's Word and praying?" Or, in other words, "How are you doing right now in your relationship with your Savior?" I appreciate Doug's question, but too often I've had to confess to my friend that I need to work on my walk.

It is within that spirit, of looking for ways to work on my walk, that this journaling workbook has been born. But it is not the reason *why* this workbook exists.

The Genesis of Psalms Journal

This workbook is a result of two adventure retreats I took in the wilderness of Utah, some twenty-five years apart. The first trip included hiking the slot canyons of the Grand Staircase-Escalante National Monument. The second was a multiday canoe trip down the Green River.

Two things tie the trips together in my mind.

First, both trips featured solo time in the profoundly stark quiet of the Utah wilderness. Second, both trips were the brainchild of my cocontributor and cousin (by marriage), Dave Tanis.

During the first trip in 1997, Dave provided the members of our group with a devotional outline we could use during our quiet time. At the bottom of the sheet was a list of eighteen psalms to consider reading. The outline's title was "Actively Acknowledging and Engaging in God's Presence." I used the outline during the trip and continued using it when I returned home. I've kept the worksheet ever since.

Fast forward twenty-five years: Dave invited me on a combination adventure/spiritual retreat to canoe Utah's Green River with a group of men. Remembering my need to improve my walk, I agreed to join the group. It was April of 2022.

I spent my solo time on that trip sitting on a mesa above a bend in the Green River. I enjoyed the protective shade of a stand of cottonwood trees, taking in the view of red-rock canyon walls around me. While journaling there, I felt a prompt from the Spirit centered on the word *writing*.

After returning home and praying for several months for clarity, I didn't feel called to write, myself. Instead, my understanding of the prompt I received is this: I believe God wants us to write—to journal, to cry out to Him from the depths of our hearts. My role is to create a tool that encourages us to write. That's *why* this journal exists.

Once my role became clear to me, I decided to expand upon the outline Dave Tanis provided us back in 1997. Consulting with Dave has proven invaluable; his years of experience leading college students on wilderness retreats provided crucial insights that support the structure of this workbook. His input has been pivotal in developing the questions included in the journaling sections.

Next, I sought the advice of my former pastor and good friend, Tim Spykstra. Tim was my pastor for seven years, and he introduced me to the idea of circling through the Psalms as

part of my daily devotions. It is only fitting that he would be involved in this project. Tim provided valuable input on the structure of the book, gave feedback on its content, and helped refine the list of psalms. He's also graciously written the foreword.

That's the backstory.

I present *Psalms Journal* to you as a friend, one who has felt compelled to share this tool with you. I hope you find it useful in your walk with God. Like any tool, its effectiveness will depend on how you put it to use. That said, I believe God is faithful and He will be there when you open His word and put pen to paper.

– *Henry Miersma*

Introduction

Introducing *Psalms Journal*

Psalms Journal is a devotional workbook that offers a guided journey through twenty-one selected psalms to help you ponder their meaning and examine their connection to your life today, all while you develop a habit of journaling and praying.

Psalms Journal invites you to meditate on one psalm each day for twenty-one straight days and guides you through the process of journaling your observations, reflections, and responses to God's Word. You'll then organize your notes and convert them into prayer prompts for praying into the day's psalm.

The goal of *Psalms Journal* is to help readers establish a habit of journaling and prayer. The concept relies on the notion that it takes three weeks to develop a new habit. Thus, twenty-one psalms. The list of included psalms is subjective and does not imply their superiority in any way.

Our ultimate goal is for you to discover the heart of the living God, to cry out to Him through journaling and prayer, and to strengthen your walk with Him.

To reach those goals, *Psalms Journal* provides a structured series of prompts guiding you through the process, including:

1. Being still and praying
2. Reading a psalm and meditating on it
3. Journaling your observations, reflections and responses to the psalm
4. Reviewing the thoughts and emotions expressed by the psalm
5. Organizing prayer points within the A.C.T.S. model and praying into the psalm

Turn the page to see an overview of the process.

The *Psalms Journal* Process

Psalms Journal allocates eight pages to each psalm, with a structured series of prompts guiding the user through the process as follows:

1

Be Still & Pray

Each day begins with two pages dedicated to helping you ***be still and pray***, focusing first on the words of Psalm 46:10, *"Be still, and know that I am God."*

The images on these pages attempt to reflect the psalm that follows, but the images themselves are not important–what is important is that you stop what you are doing and focus your attention on God (I recommend leaving your phone elsewhere).

As you settle into your space, lift up a prayer and ask God to send His Holy Spirit to speak to you through His Word and help you hear His voice.

2

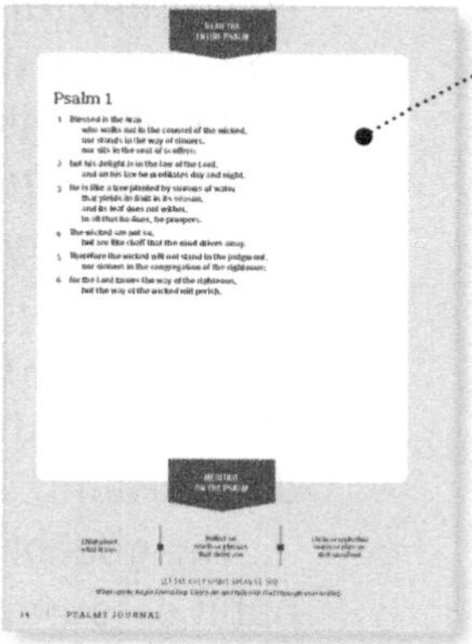

Read & Meditate

Next, the third page presents the psalm and invites the user to ***read and meditate*** on what the psalm says.

Reflect on words or phrases that strike you; circle or underline words or phrases that stand out. *Let the Holy Spirit speak to you through His Word.*

ABOUT THE PROCESS

Prayer Points:

As you progress through the pages allocated to a psalm, convert selected reflections, journal highlights and/or "additional thoughts for prayer" into **prayer points** and organize them within the A.C.T.S. model on the final page.

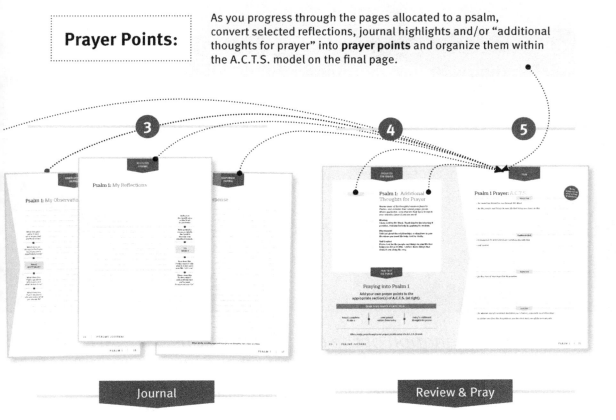

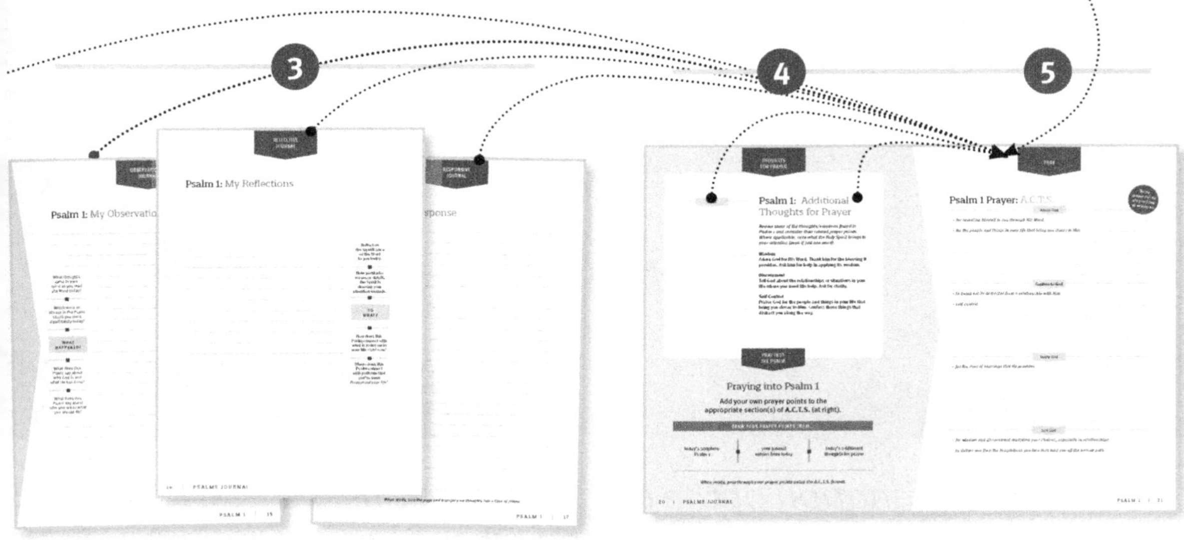

Journal

Three pages are provided each day for the ***journaling*** portion of the process. There is one page each for observational, reflective, and responsive journaling. The prompts found on these pages include: *Which word or phrase in the psalm struck you most significantly today? How does this psalm connect with what is going on in your life right now?*

You can find expanded instructions for the three sections of journaling on pages 16-17.

Review & Pray

Each day ends with two pages dedicated to ***prayer.***

First, in the "Additional Thoughts for Prayer" section, you are invited to review some of the thoughts and emotions expressed in the psalm and their related prayer points.

Next, you are prompted to organize your prayer efforts by adding prayer points into the appropriate section of the **A.C.T.S.** format on the final page. Prayer points are drawn from the psalm itself, the day's journal entries, and the "Additional Thoughts for Prayer" section.

Finally, bring everything from the day's session to God in prayer.

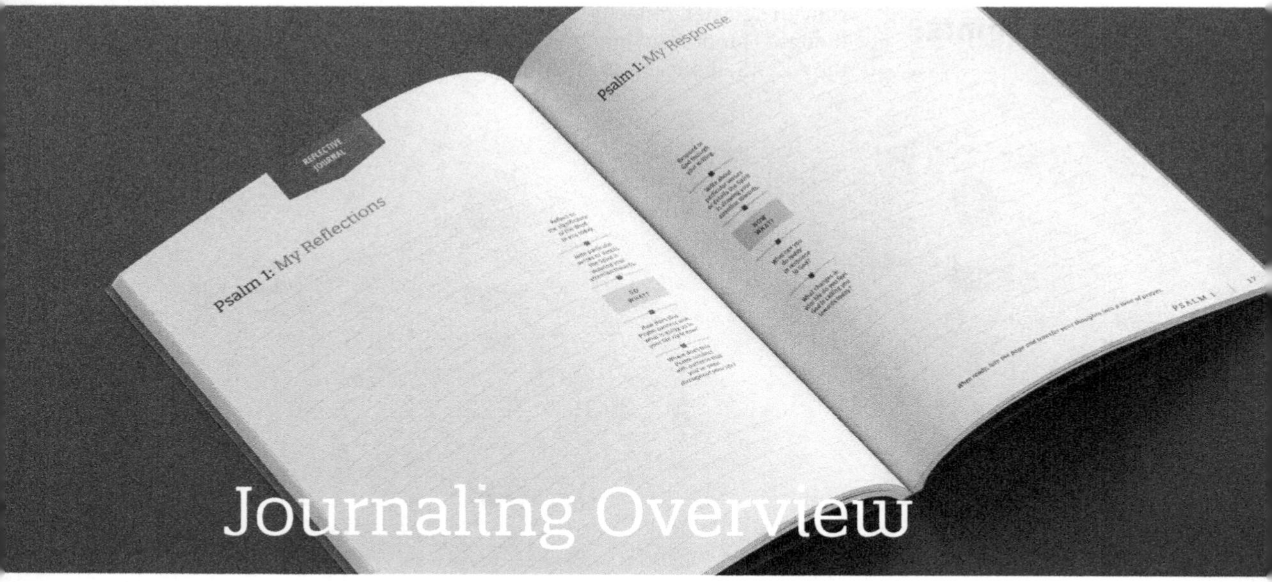

Journaling Overview

An explanation of the differences between observational, reflective, and responsive journaling.

Psalms Journal invites you to journal as a means to experience God's Word in deeper ways. In a culture that embraces short texts, we are less practiced in exploring our thoughts through writing. There are many models that provide a framework for journaling. Since this project was conceived on an adventure trip, it is appropriate to use a model from the field of adventure education.

I was first introduced to the "What? So What? Now What?" framework through literature produced by Project Adventure. It finds its foundation in the work of American educator John Dewey who emphasized the importance of reflection in making meaning (or learning) from experiences. *Psalms Journal* uses this framework to help us reflect and learn from the Psalms.

This is a dynamic process that invites you to not only engage the text but do so in the context of your lived experience. What is God doing in your life right now and how does that intersect with the psalm before you? I believe that working through this journal a year from now will yield very different observations, reflections, and responses. God's Word is dynamic and speaks to us differently at various times in our lives.

On the "My Observations" journal page, you are invited to engage with the psalm by noting *what* is in the passage: circling words that jump out to you, identifying what the psalm says about God's character, etc. In this section, you are primarily observing, but you will note what the Holy Spirit is bringing to your attention at this specific time in your life. During this stage of journaling, give freedom to your reactions, intuition, and impulses. The Holy Spirit may be drawing your attention to certain aspects of the psalm; don't thwart that process by trying to understand why you are being drawn to certain words or phrases (this occurs in the next journaling section). Trust that God's Word can speak into your life and note how you are responding to it in this moment.

The "My Reflections" journal page is an opportunity for you to identify *why* the Holy Spirit is bringing these things to your attention (the "so what?"). In the observation section, certain words or phrases may have stood out to you. In this section, try to discern why this is, considering your current life situation or events from your past. Our lives are stories that God is writing, and His Word may resonate with us in unique ways. Why are aspects of this psalm connecting with your story at this moment? The primary goal of this section is not to find the "correct" answer to this question but to use journaling to explore your thoughts and feelings from your encounter with this psalm.

On the "My Response" journal page, we explore ways we might *respond* to our encounter with the psalm. This is the "now what?" section. As Christians, we are saved by grace through faith in Jesus Christ. A faithful response to God's gift of grace is thanksgiving, and it is out of thanksgiving that we do the "good work" of loving God and loving our neighbor. And so, our engagement with the psalm should lead us to respond in tangible acts of love for God and for our neighbor. In this section, let your journaling help you explore ways the Holy Spirit might be prompting you to respond based on your observation and reflections on the psalm.

Our hope is that the process of observational, reflective, and responsive journaling will help you experience God's Word in deep, significant, and tangible ways. We pray you will come to experience God's heart for you as you become more aware of the ways He is walking with you today and has been walking with you throughout your life.

– Dave Tanis, D. Ed

DAY 1

Psalm 1

"Be still, and know that I am God"
– Psalm 46:10

■

Be settled physically
(but not too comfortable)

■

Ask the Holy Spirit to work in you
as you read God's Word

When ready, turn the page and read the entire psalm.

READ THE ENTIRE PSALM

Psalm 1

1 Blessed is the man
who walks not in the counsel of the wicked,
nor stands in the way of sinners,
nor sits in the seat of scoffers;
2 but his delight is in the law of the Lord,
and on his law he meditates day and night.
3 He is like a tree planted by streams of water
that yields its fruit in its season,
and its leaf does not wither.
In all that he does, he prospers.
4 The wicked are not so,
but are like chaff that the wind drives away.
5 Therefore the wicked will not stand in the judgment,
nor sinners in the congregation of the righteous;
6 for the Lord knows the way of the righteous,
but the way of the wicked will perish.

MEDITATE ON THE PSALM

Think about what it says

Reflect on words or phrases that strike you

Circle or underline words or phrases that stand out

LET THE HOLY SPIRIT SPEAK TO YOU

When ready, begin journaling. Listen for and talk with God through your writing.

Psalm 1: My Observations

What thoughts came to your mind as you read the Word today?

Which word or phrase in the psalm struck you most significantly today?

WHAT HAPPENED?

What does this psalm say about who God is and what He has done?

What does this psalm say about who you are or what you should do?

Psalm 1: My Reflections

Reflect on
the significance
of the Word
to you today.

Reflect on why you
think the Spirit has
drawn you to certain
verses or details
in this psalm.

**SO
WHAT?**

How does this
psalm connect with
what is going on in
your life *right now*?

Where does this
psalm connect
with patterns that
you've seen
throughout your life?

Psalm 1: My Response

Respond to God through your writing.

Write about particular verses or details the Spirit is drawing your attention toward.

NOW WHAT?

What can you do *today* in response to God?

What changes in your life do you feel God is calling you to make today?

When ready, turn the page and begin a time of prayer based on these observations, reflections and responses.

THOUGHTS FOR PRAYER

Notes

Psalm 1: Additional Thoughts for Prayer

Review some of the thoughts and emotions found in Psalm 1 and consider their related prayer points. Where applicable, note what the Holy Spirit brings to your attention (even if just one word).

Wisdom
Adore God for His Word. Thank Him for the blessing it provides. Ask Him for help to apply its wisdom.

Discernment
Tell God about the relationships or situations in your life where you need His help. Ask for clarity.

Self-Control
Praise God for the people and things in your life that bring you closer to Him. Confess those things that distract you along the way.

PRAY INTO THE PSALM

Praying into Psalm 1

Add your own prayer points to the appropriate section(s) of A.C.T.S. (at right).

DRAW YOUR PRAYER POINTS FROM...

today's scripture: Psalm 1

your journal entries from today

today's additional thoughts for prayer

When ready, pray through your prayer points using the A.C.T.S. format.

Psalm 1 Prayer: A.C.T.S.

Some prayer points are provided as examples

Adore God

– for revealing Himself to you through His Word

– for the people and things in your life that bring you closer to Him

Confess to God

– that you are easily distracted from a relationship with Him

– your lack of self-control

Thank God

– for the river of blessings that He provides

Ask God

– for wisdom and discernment regarding your choices, especially in relationships

– to deliver you from the temptations you face that lead you off the narrow path

DAY 2

Psalm 8

"Be still, and know that I am God"
– Psalm 46:10

■

Be settled physically
(but not too comfortable)

■

Ask the Holy Spirit to work in you
as you read God's Word

When ready, turn the page and read the entire psalm.

READ THE ENTIRE PSALM

Psalm 8

1 O Lord, our Lord,
how majestic is your name in all the earth!
You have set your glory above the heavens.

2 Out of the mouth of babies and infants,
you have established strength because of your foes,
to still the enemy and the avenger.

3 When I look at your heavens, the work of your fingers,
the moon and the stars, which you have set in place,

4 what is man that you are mindful of him,
and the son of man that you care for him?

5 Yet you have made him a little lower
than the heavenly beings
and crowned him with glory and honor.

6 You have given him dominion over the works of your hands;
you have put all things under his feet,

7 all sheep and oxen,
and also the beasts of the field,

8 the birds of the heavens, and the fish of the sea,
whatever passes along the paths of the seas.

9 O Lord, our Lord,
how majestic is your name in all the earth!

MEDITATE ON THE PSALM

Think about what it says | Reflect on words or phrases that strike you | Circle or underline words or phrases that stand out

LET THE HOLY SPIRIT SPEAK TO YOU

When ready, begin journaling. Listen for and talk with God through your writing.

OBSERVATIONAL JOURNAL

Psalm 8: My Observations

What thoughts came to your mind as you read the Word today?

Which word or phrase in the psalm struck you most significantly today?

WHAT HAPPENED?

What does this psalm say about who God is and what He has done?

What does this psalm say about who you are or what you should do?

Psalm 8: My Reflections

Reflect on the significance of the Word to you today.

Reflect on why you think the Spirit has drawn you to certain verses or details in this psalm.

SO WHAT?

How does this psalm connect with what is going on in your life *right now*?

Where does this psalm connect with patterns that you've seen *throughout your life*?

Psalm 8: My Response

Respond to God through your writing.

Write about particular verses or details the Spirit is drawing your attention toward.

NOW WHAT?

What can you do *today* in response to God?

What changes in your life do you feel God is calling you to make today?

When ready, turn the page and begin a time of prayer based on these observations, reflections and responses.

THOUGHTS FOR PRAYER

Notes

Psalm 8: Additional Thoughts for Prayer

Review some of the thoughts and emotions found in Psalm 8 and consider their related prayer points. Where applicable, note what the Holy Spirit brings to your attention (even if just one word).

Lord
Adore and thank God for His lordship. Is there any portion of your life that you have not fully given over to Him? Confess that to Him.

Glory
What comes into your mind as you consider God's glory? Ask Him to show you His glory.

Provision
Thank God for caring about you. Specify how you experience His mindfulness of you.

PRAY INTO THE PSALM

Praying into Psalm 8

Add your own prayer points to the appropriate section(s) of A.C.T.S. (at right).

DRAW YOUR PRAYER POINTS FROM...

today's scripture: Psalm 8	your journal entries from today	today's additional thoughts for prayer

When ready, pray through your prayer points using the A.C.T.S. format.

Some prayer points are provided as examples

Psalm 8 Prayer: A.C.T.S.

Adore God

– *for being Lord of your life*

– *for how He reveals His majesty to you.*

Confess to God

– *where you need help in having Him be Lord of your life*

– *your inability to fully comprehend and appreciate Him*

Thank God

– *for revealing Himself to you through creation*

– *for His grace in making you a little lower than the heavenly beings*

– *for His grace in giving you dominion over the works of His hands*

Ask God

– *for the words to speak to tell others about Him*

– *to deliver you from the temptations you face that lead you off the narrow path*

DAY 3

Psalm 19

"Be still, and know that I am God"
– Psalm 46:10

■

Be settled physically
(but not too comfortable)

■

Ask the Holy Spirit to work in you
as you read God's Word

When ready, turn the page and read the entire psalm.

READ THE
ENTIRE PSALM

Psalm 19

1 The heavens declare the glory
of God, and the sky above
proclaims his handiwork.

2 Day to day pours out speech, and
night to night reveals knowledge.

3 There is no speech, nor are there
words, whose voice is not heard.

4 Their voice goes out through all the
earth, and their words to the end
of the world. In them he has set a
tent for the sun,

5 which comes out like a bridegroom
leaving his chamber, and,
like a strong man, runs its
course with joy.

6 Its rising is from the end of
the heavens, and its circuit to the
end of them, and there is nothing
hidden from its heat.

7 The law of the Lord is perfect,
reviving the soul;
the testimony of the Lord is sure,
making wise the simple;

8 the precepts of the Lord are right,
rejoicing the heart;
the commandment of the Lord is
pure, enlightening the eyes;

9 the fear of the Lord is clean,
enduring forever;
the rules of the Lord are true,
and righteous altogether.

10 More to be desired are they than
gold, even much fine gold;
sweeter also than honey and
drippings of the honeycomb.

11 Moreover, by them is your servant
warned; in keeping them there
is great reward.

12 Who can discern his errors? Declare
me innocent from hidden faults.

13 Keep back your servant also
from presumptuous sins;
let them not have dominion
over me! Then I shall be
blameless, and innocent of
great transgression.

14 Let the words of my mouth and
the meditation of my heart
be acceptable in your sight,
O Lord, my rock and my redeemer.

MEDITATE
ON THE PSALM

Think about what it says | Reflect on words or phrases that strike you | Circle or underline words or phrases that stand out

LET THE HOLY SPIRIT SPEAK TO YOU

When ready, begin journaling. Listen for and talk with God through your writing.

Psalm 19: My Observations

What thoughts came to your mind as you read the Word today?

Which word or phrase in the psalm struck you most significantly today?

WHAT HAPPENED?

What does this psalm say about who God is and what He has done?

What does this psalm say about who you are or what you should do?

Psalm 19: My Reflections

Reflect on the significance of the Word to you today.

Reflect on why you think the Spirit has drawn you to certain verses or details in this psalm.

SO WHAT?

How does this psalm connect with what is going on in your life *right now*?

Where does this psalm connect with patterns that you've seen *throughout your life*?

Psalm 19: My Response

Respond to God through your writing.

Write about particular verses or details the Spirit is drawing your attention toward.

NOW WHAT?

What can you do *today* in response to God?

What changes in your life do you feel God is calling you to make today?

When ready, turn the page and begin a time of prayer based on these observations, reflections and responses.

THOUGHTS FOR PRAYER

Notes

Psalm 19: Additional Thoughts for Prayer

Review some of the thoughts and emotions found in Psalm 19 and consider their related prayer points. Where applicable, note what the Holy Spirit brings to your attention (even if just one word).

Majesty
Adore His name and His beauty. Note some of the ways God reveals His majesty to you personally.

Direction
Thank God for providing direction for your life through His Word. Tell Him about specific needs or concerns you have.

Perseverance
Ask Him for strength. Give Him anything that might be making you feel weary today.

PRAY INTO THE PSALM

Praying into Psalm 19

Add your own prayer points to the appropriate section(s) of A.C.T.S. (at right).

DRAW YOUR PRAYER POINTS FROM...

today's scripture: Psalm 19	your journal entries from today	today's additional thoughts for prayer

When ready, pray through your prayer points using the A.C.T.S. format.

Psalm 19 Prayer: A.C.T.S.

Some prayer points are provided as examples

Adore God

– *for His amazing creation*

– *for particular places or aspects of His creation that you love*

– *for what you know about Him as revealed to you through His creation*

Confess to God

– *your idols, the things you value more than Him*

– *your need for His mercy and grace*

Thank God

– *for revealing Himself to you through His Word*

– *for revealing Himself to you through His creation*

– *for being your rock and redeemer*

Ask God

– *to guide your heart, mind and speech, that they would be acceptable to Him*

– *to guide the words you speak in order to reflect and glorify Him in your life*

DAY 4

Psalm 22

"Be still, and know that I am God"
– Psalm 46:10

■

Be settled physically
(but not too comfortable)

■

Ask the Holy Spirit to work in you
as you read God's Word

When ready, turn the page and read the entire psalm.

READ THE ENTIRE PSALM

Psalm 22

1 My God, my God, why have you forsaken me?
Why are you so far from saving me,
from the words of my groaning?
2 O my God, I cry by day, but you do not answer,
and by night, but I find no rest.
3 Yet you are holy, enthroned on
the praises of Israel.
4 In you our fathers trusted;
they trusted, and you delivered them.
5 To you they cried and were rescued; in you they
trusted and were not put to shame.
6 But I am a worm and not a man, scorned
by mankind and despised by the people.
7 All who see me mock me; they make mouths
at me; they wag their heads;
8 "He trusts in the Lord; let him deliver him;
let him rescue him, for he delights in him!"
9 Yet you are he who took me from the womb;
you made me trust you at my mother's breasts.
10 On you was I cast from my birth, and from my
mother's womb you have been my God.
11 Be not far from me, for trouble is near,
and there is none to help.
12 Many bulls encompass me;
strong bulls of Bashan surround me;
13 they open wide their mouths at me,
like a ravening and roaring lion.
14 I am poured out like water, and all my bones are
out of joint; my heart is like wax; it is melted
within my breast;
15 my strength is dried up like a potsherd,
and my tongue sticks to my jaws;
you lay me in the dust of death.
16 For dogs encompass me;
a company of evildoers encircles me;
they have pierced my hands and feet—
17 I can count all my bones—they stare and gloat
over me;
18 they divide my garments among them,
and for my clothing they cast lots.
19 But you, O Lord, do not be far off! O you my help,
come quickly to my aid!
20 Deliver my soul from the sword, my precious
life from the power of the dog!
21 Save me from the mouth of the lion! You have
rescued me from the horns of the wild oxen!
22 I will tell of your name to my brothers; in the
midst of the congregation I will praise you:
23 You who fear the Lord, praise him!
All you offspring of Jacob, glorify him, and
stand in awe of him, all you offspring of Israel!
24 For he has not despised or abhorred the
affliction of the afflicted, and he has not
hidden his face from him, but has heard,
when he cried to him.
25 From you comes my praise in the great
congregation; my vows I will perform
before those who fear him.
26 The afflicted shall eat and be satisfied;
those who seek him shall praise the Lord!
May your hearts live forever!
27 All the ends of the earth shall remember and
turn to the Lord, and all the families of
the nations shall worship before you.
28 For kingship belongs to the Lord,
and he rules over the nations.
29 All the prosperous of the earth eat and worship;
before him shall bow all who go
down to the dust, even the one who
could not keep himself alive.
30 Posterity shall serve him; it shall be told of the
Lord to the coming generation;
31 they shall come and proclaim his righteousness
to a people yet unborn, that he has done it.

MEDITATE ON THE PSALM

Think about what it says

Reflect on words or phrases that strike you

Circle or underline words or phrases that stand out

LET THE HOLY SPIRIT SPEAK TO YOU

When ready, begin journaling. Listen for and talk with God through your writing.

Psalm 22: My Observations

What thoughts came to your mind as you read the Word today?

Which word or phrase in the psalm struck you most significantly today?

WHAT HAPPENED?

What does this psalm say about who God is and what He has done?

What does this psalm say about who you are or what you should do?

Psalm 22: My Reflections

Reflect on the significance of the Word to you today.

Reflect on why you think the Spirit has drawn you to certain verses or details in this psalm.

SO WHAT?

How does this psalm connect with what is going on in your life *right now*?

Where does this psalm connect with patterns that you've seen *throughout your life*?

Psalm 22: My Response

Respond to God through your writing.

Write about particular verses or details the Spirit is drawing your attention toward.

NOW WHAT?

What can you do *today* in response to God?

What changes in your life do you feel God is calling you to make today?

When ready, turn the page and begin a time of prayer based on these observations, reflections and responses.

THOUGHTS
FOR PRAYER

Notes

Psalm 22: Additional Thoughts for Prayer

Review some of the thoughts and emotions found in Psalm 22 and consider their related prayer points. Where applicable, note what the Holy Spirit brings to your attention (even if just one word).

Distant
If you feel like God is far away, tell Him.
Ask Him to draw near to you and speak to your heart.
Give your "Why, God?" questions to Him.

Trust
Thank God for specific examples in your life that remind you He is worthy of your trust.

Hope
Adore Him as King. Praise Him for the hope you have in Him because He is your King. Who do you know that needs this hope? Pray for them.

PRAY INTO
THE PSALM

Praying into Psalm 22

Add your own prayer points to the appropriate section(s) of A.C.T.S. (at right).

DRAW YOUR PRAYER POINTS FROM...

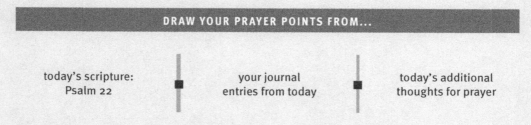

today's scripture: Psalm 22	your journal entries from today	today's additional thoughts for prayer

When ready, pray through your prayer points using the A.C.T.S. format.

Psalm 22 Prayer: A.C.T.S.

Adore God

Confess to God

Thank God

Ask God

DAY 5

Psalm 23

"Be still, and know that I am God"
– Psalm 46:10

■

Be settled physically
(but not too comfortable)

■

Ask the Holy Spirit to work in you
as you read God's Word

When ready, turn the page and read the entire psalm.

READ THE ENTIRE PSALM

Psalm 23

1 The Lord is my shepherd;
I shall not want.

2 He makes me lie down in green pastures.
He leads me beside still waters.
He restores my soul.

3 He leads me in paths of righteousness
for his name's sake.

4 Even though I walk through the valley
of the shadow of death,
I will fear no evil,
for you are with me;
your rod and your staff,
they comfort me.

5 You prepare a table before me
in the presence of my enemies;
you anoint my head with oil;
my cup overflows.

6 Surely goodness and mercy
shall follow me all the days of my life,
and I shall dwell in the house
of the Lord forever.

MEDITATE ON THE PSALM

Think about what it says | Reflect on words or phrases that strike you | Circle or underline words or phrases that stand out

LET THE HOLY SPIRIT SPEAK TO YOU

When ready, begin journaling. Listen for and talk with God through your writing.

Psalm 23: My Observations

What thoughts came to your mind as you read the Word today?

Which word or phrase in the psalm struck you most significantly today?

WHAT HAPPENED?

What does this psalm say about who God is and what He has done?

What does this psalm say about who you are or what you should do?

Psalm 23: My Reflections

Reflect on the significance of the Word to you today.

Reflect on why you think the Spirit has drawn you to certain verses or details in this psalm.

SO WHAT?

How does this psalm connect with what is going on in your life *right now*?

Where does this psalm connect with patterns that you've seen *throughout your life*?

Psalm 23: My Response

Respond to God through your writing.

Write about particular verses or details the Spirit is drawing your attention toward.

NOW WHAT?

What can you do *today* in response to God?

What changes in your life do you feel God is calling you to make today?

When ready, turn the page and begin a time of prayer based on these observations, reflections and responses.

THOUGHTS FOR PRAYER

Notes

Psalm 23: Additional Thoughts for Prayer

Review some of the thoughts and emotions found in Psalm 23 and consider their related prayer points. Where applicable, note what the Holy Spirit brings to your attention (even if just one word).

Shepherd
Adore Him as your trustworthy shepherd. Ask Him to help you hear His voice clearly.

Guidance
Thank God for His Word. Tell Him about specific needs you have for His guidance and ask for His help.

Provision
Adore Him for His provision in your life. Praise Him for specific ways you've seen His hand provide.
Lay your needs at His feet.

PRAY INTO THE PSALM

Praying into Psalm 23

Add your own prayer points to the appropriate section(s) of A.C.T.S. (at right).

DRAW YOUR PRAYER POINTS FROM...

today's scripture: Psalm 23	your journal entries from today	today's additional thoughts for prayer

When ready, pray through your prayer points using the A.C.T.S. format.

Psalm 23 Prayer: A.C.T.S.

Adore God

Confess to God

Thank God

Ask God

DAY 6

Psalm 24

"Be still, and know that I am God"
– Psalm 46:10

■

Be settled physically
(but not too comfortable)

■

Ask the Holy Spirit to work in you
as you read God's Word

When ready, turn the page and read the entire psalm.

READ THE ENTIRE PSALM

Psalm 24

1 The earth is the Lord's and the fullness thereof,
the world and those who dwell therein,
2 for he has founded it upon the seas
and established it upon the rivers.
3 Who shall ascend the hill of the Lord?
And who shall stand in his holy place?
4 He who has clean hands and a pure heart,
who does not lift up his soul to what is false
and does not swear deceitfully.
5 He will receive blessing from the Lord
and righteousness from the God of his salvation.
6 Such is the generation of those who seek him,
who seek the face of the God of Jacob. *Selah*
7 Lift up your heads, O gates!
And be lifted up, O ancient doors,
that the King of glory may come in.
8 Who is this King of glory?
The Lord, strong and mighty,
the Lord, mighty in battle!
9 Lift up your heads, O gates!
And lift them up, O ancient doors,
that the King of glory may come in.
10 Who is this King of glory?
The Lord of hosts,
he is the King of glory! *Selah*

MEDITATE ON THE PSALM

Think about what it says

Reflect on words or phrases that strike you

Circle or underline words or phrases that stand out

LET THE HOLY SPIRIT SPEAK TO YOU

When ready, begin journaling. Listen for and talk with God through your writing.

Psalm 24: My Observations

What thoughts came to your mind as you read the Word today?

Which word or phrase in the psalm struck you most significantly today?

WHAT HAPPENED?

What does this psalm say about who God is and what He has done?

What does this psalm say about who you are or what you should do?

Psalm 24: My Reflections

Reflect on the significance of the Word to you today.

Reflect on why you think the Spirit has drawn you to certain verses or details in this psalm.

SO WHAT?

How does this psalm connect with what is going on in your life *right now*?

Where does this psalm connect with patterns that you've seen *throughout your life*?

Psalm 24: My Response

Respond to God through your writing.

Write about particular verses or details the Spirit is drawing your attention toward.

NOW WHAT?

What can you do *today* in response to God?

What changes in your life do you feel God is calling you to make today?

When ready, turn the page and begin a time of prayer based on these observations, reflections and responses.

THOUGHTS FOR PRAYER

Notes

Psalm 24: Additional Thoughts for Prayer

Review some of the thoughts and emotions found in Psalm 24 and consider their related prayer points. Where applicable, note what the Holy Spirit brings to your attention (even if just one word).

Kingship
Adore God as your creator King. Consider what "the fullness thereof" means to you and thank Him.

Holiness
Adore His holiness. Tell Him about specific situations where you need His help to guard your heart. Ask for His help.

Glory
Adore Him for His glory. Give specific example of how God reveals His glory to you.

PRAY INTO THE PSALM

Praying into Psalm 24

Add your own prayer points to the appropriate section(s) of A.C.T.S. (at right).

DRAW YOUR PRAYER POINTS FROM...

today's scripture: Psalm 24

your journal entries from today

today's additional thoughts for prayer

When ready, pray through your prayer points using the A.C.T.S. format.

Psalm 24 Prayer: A.C.T.S.

Adore God

Confess to God

Thank God

Ask God

DAY 7

Psalm 27

"Be still, and know that I am God"
– Psalm 46:10

■

Be settled physically
(but not too comfortable)

■

Ask the Holy Spirit to work in you
as you read God's Word

When ready, turn the page and read the entire psalm.

READ THE ENTIRE PSALM

Psalm 27

1 The Lord is my light and my salvation;
whom shall I fear? The Lord is the
stronghold of my life; of whom
shall I be afraid?

2 When evildoers assail me to eat up
my flesh, my adversaries and foes,
it is they who stumble and fall.

3 Though an army encamp against me,
my heart shall not fear,
though war arise against me,
yet I will be confident.

4 One thing have I asked of the Lord,
that will I seek after: that I may
dwell in the house of the Lord all
the days of my life, to gaze upon
the beauty of the Lord and to
inquire in his temple.

5 For he will hide me in his shelter in
the day of trouble; he will conceal
me under the cover of his tent;
he will lift me high upon a rock.

6 And now my head shall be lifted up
above my enemies all around me,
and I will offer in his tent sacrifices
with shouts of joy; I will sing and
make melody to the Lord.

7 Hear, O Lord, when I cry aloud; be
gracious to me and answer me!

8 You have said, "Seek my face."
My heart says to you, "Your face,
Lord, do I seek."

9 Hide not your face from me. Turn not
your servant away in anger,
O you who have been my help.
Cast me not off; forsake me not,
O God of my salvation!

10 For my father and my mother
have forsaken me, but the Lord
will take me in.

11 Teach me your way, O Lord,
and lead me on a level path
because of my enemies.

12 Give me not up to the will of my
adversaries; for false witnesses
have risen against me, and they
breathe out violence.

13 I believe that I shall look upon
the goodness of the Lord in
the land of the living!

14 Wait for the Lord; be strong,
and let your heart take courage;
wait for the Lord!

MEDITATE ON THE PSALM

Think about what it says

Reflect on words or phrases that strike you

Circle or underline words or phrases that stand out

LET THE HOLY SPIRIT SPEAK TO YOU

When ready, begin journaling. Listen for and talk with God through your writing.

Psalm 27: My Observations

What thoughts came to your mind as you read the Word today?

Which word or phrase in the psalm struck you most significantly today?

WHAT HAPPENED?

What does this psalm say about who God is and what He has done?

What does this psalm say about who you are or what you should do?

Psalm 27: My Reflections

Reflect on the significance of the Word to you today.

Reflect on why you think the Spirit has drawn you to certain verses or details in this psalm.

SO WHAT?

How does this psalm connect with what is going on in your life *right now*?

Where does this psalm connect with patterns that you've seen *throughout your life*?

Psalm 27: My Response

Respond to God through your writing.

Write about particular verses or details the Spirit is drawing your attention toward.

NOW WHAT?

What can you do *today* in response to God?

What changes in your life do you feel God is calling you to make today?

When ready, turn the page and begin a time of prayer based on these observations, reflections and responses.

THOUGHTS FOR PRAYER

Notes

Psalm 27: Additional Thoughts for Prayer

Review some of the thoughts and emotions found in Psalm 27 and consider their related prayer points. Where applicable, note what the Holy Spirit brings to your attention (even if just one word).

Strength
Adore God for His strength. Tell Him about the adversities you face and give them to Him. Ask Him to strengthen your spirit.

Trust
Adore God for being trustworthy. If you have doubts, tell Him your specific needs.

Perseverance
Are you wrestling with God's timing in your life? Is there something you desperately wish would happen that hasn't come to fruition? Tell God how you feel. Ask Him what He wants you to learn or understand.

PRAY INTO THE PSALM

Praying into Psalm 27

Add your own prayer points to the appropriate section(s) of A.C.T.S. (at right).

DRAW YOUR PRAYER POINTS FROM...

today's scripture: Psalm 27	your journal entries from today	today's additional thoughts for prayer

When ready, pray through your prayer points using the A.C.T.S. format.

Psalm 27 Prayer: A.C.T.S.

Adore God

Confess to God

Thank God

Ask God

DAY 8

Psalm 32

BE STILL & PRAY

"Be still, and know that I am God"
– Psalm 46:10

■

Be settled physically
(but not too comfortable)

■

Ask the Holy Spirit to work in you
as you read God's Word

When ready, turn the page and read the entire psalm.

READ THE ENTIRE PSALM

Psalm 32

1 Blessed is the one whose transgression is forgiven,
whose sin is covered.

2 Blessed is the man against whom
the Lord counts no iniquity,
and in whose spirit there is no deceit.

3 For when I kept silent, my bones wasted away
through my groaning all day long.

4 For day and night your hand was
heavy upon me; my strength was dried up
as by the heat of summer. *Selah*

5 I acknowledged my sin to you,
and I did not cover my iniquity; I said,
"I will confess my transgressions to the Lord,"
and you forgave the iniquity of my sin. *Selah*

6 Therefore let everyone who is godly offer prayer to
you at a time when you may be found; surely in the rush
of great waters, they shall not reach him.

7 You are a hiding place for me; you preserve me from trouble;
you surround me with shouts of deliverance. *Selah*

8 I will instruct you and teach you in the way you should go;
I will counsel you with my eye upon you.

9 Be not like a horse or a mule, without understanding,
which must be curbed with bit and bridle,
or it will not stay near you.

10 Many are the sorrows of the wicked,
but steadfast love surrounds the one
who trusts in the Lord.

11 Be glad in the Lord, and rejoice, O righteous,
and shout for joy, all you upright in heart!

MEDITATE ON THE PSALM

Think about what it says | Reflect on words or phrases that strike you | Circle or underline words or phrases that stand out

LET THE HOLY SPIRIT SPEAK TO YOU

When ready, begin journaling. Listen for and talk with God through your writing.

Psalm 32: My Observations

What thoughts came to your mind as you read the Word today?

Which word or phrase in the psalm struck you most significantly today?

WHAT HAPPENED?

What does this psalm say about who God is and what He has done?

What does this psalm say about who you are or what you should do?

Psalm 32: My Reflections

Reflect on the significance of the Word to you today.

Reflect on why you think the Spirit has drawn you to certain verses or details in this psalm.

SO WHAT?

How does this psalm connect with what is going on in your life *right now*?

Where does this psalm connect with patterns that you've seen *throughout your life*?

Psalm 32: My Response

Respond to
God through
your writing.

Write about
particular verses
or details the Spirit
is drawing your
attention toward.

**NOW
WHAT?**

What can you
do *today*
in response
to God?

What changes in
your life do you feel
God is calling you
to make today?

When ready, turn the page and begin a time of prayer based on these observations, reflections and responses.

THOUGHTS FOR PRAYER

Notes

Psalm 32: Additional Thoughts for Prayer

Review some of the thoughts and emotions found in Psalm 32 and consider their related prayer points. Where applicable, note what the Holy Spirit brings to your attention (even if just one word).

Blessed
Thank God for the gift of His Son and the greatest blessing of all, your salvation though Him.

Confession
Do you ever "cover" your iniquity? Acknowledge your sins to Him. Thank Him for His forgiveness and the peace He provides.

Stubbornness
"Be not like a horse or a mule" (verse 9). Have you ever thought about that verse and whether it applies to you? Are you wrestling with unconfessed sin? Tell God about it. Ask Him for His forgiveness and His joy.

PRAY INTO THE PSALM

Praying into Psalm 32

Add your own prayer points to the appropriate section(s) of A.C.T.S. (at right).

DRAW YOUR PRAYER POINTS FROM...

today's scripture: Psalm 32	your journal entries from today	today's additional thoughts for prayer

When ready, pray through your prayer points using the A.C.T.S. format.

Psalm 32 Prayer: A.C.T.S.

Adore God

Confess to God

Thank God

Ask God

DAY 9

Psalm 33

"Be still, and know that I am God"
– Psalm 46:10

■

Be settled physically
(but not too comfortable)

■

Ask the Holy Spirit to work in you
as you read God's Word

When ready, turn the page and read the entire psalm.

READ THE ENTIRE PSALM

Psalm 33

1 Shout for joy in the Lord, O you righteous!
Praise befits the upright.

2 Give thanks to the Lord with the lyre;
make melody to him with
the harp of ten strings!

3 Sing to him a new song; play skillfully
on the strings, with loud shouts.

4 For the word of the Lord is upright,
and all his work is done in faithfulness.

5 He loves righteousness and justice;
the earth is full of the steadfast
love of the Lord.

6 By the word of the Lord the heavens
were made, and by the breath of
his mouth all their host.

7 He gathers the waters of the sea as a heap;
he puts the deeps in storehouses.

8 Let all the earth fear the Lord;
let all the inhabitants of the world
stand in awe of him!

9 For he spoke, and it came to be;
he commanded, and it stood firm.

10 The Lord brings the counsel of
the nations to nothing; he frustrates
the plans of the peoples.

11 The counsel of the Lord stands forever,
the plans of his heart to all generations.

12 Blessed is the nation whose God
is the Lord, the people whom he
has chosen as his heritage!

13 The Lord looks down from heaven;
he sees all the children of man;

14 from where he sits enthroned he looks out
on all the inhabitants of the earth,

15 he who fashions the hearts of them all
and observes all their deeds.

16 The king is not saved by his great army;
a warrior is not delivered
by his great strength.

17 The war horse is a false hope for salvation,
and by its great might it cannot rescue.

18 Behold, the eye of the Lord is on those
who fear him, on those who hope in his
steadfast love,

19 that he may deliver their soul from death
and keep them alive in famine.

20 Our soul waits for the Lord;
he is our help and our shield.

21 For our heart is glad in him,
because we trust in his holy name.

22 Let your steadfast love, O Lord,
be upon us, even as we hope in you.

MEDITATE ON THE PSALM

Think about what it says

Reflect on words or phrases that strike you

Circle or underline words or phrases that stand out

LET THE HOLY SPIRIT SPEAK TO YOU

When ready, begin journaling. Listen for and talk with God through your writing.

Psalm 33: My Observations

What thoughts came to your mind as you read the Word today?

Which word or phrase in the psalm struck you most significantly today?

WHAT HAPPENED?

What does this psalm say about who God is and what He has done?

What does this psalm say about who you are or what you should do?

Psalm 33: My Reflections

Reflect on the significance of the Word to you today.

Reflect on why you think the Spirit has drawn you to certain verses or details in this psalm.

SO WHAT?

How does this psalm connect with what is going on in your life *right now*?

Where does this psalm connect with patterns that you've seen *throughout your life*?

Psalm 33: My Response

Respond to God through your writing.

Write about particular verses or details the Spirit is drawing your attention toward.

NOW WHAT?

What can you do *today* in response to God?

What changes in your life do you feel God is calling you to make today?

When ready, turn the page and begin a time of prayer based on these observations, reflections and responses.

THOUGHTS FOR PRAYER

Notes

Psalm 33: Additional Thoughts for Prayer

Review some of the thoughts and emotions found in Psalm 33 and consider their related prayer points. Where applicable, note what the Holy Spirit brings to your attention (even if just one word).

Praise
Sing or speak the words of the "Doxology":
Praise God from whom all blessings flow, Praise him all creatures here below; Praise him above, ye heav'nly hosts; Praise Father, Son and Holy Ghost. Amen.

Security
What is your "great army"? What are you relying on in this world other than God? Tell Him about it. Thank Him for His promise of deliverance.

Hope
Is your heart "glad in him" today? Tell God about it. Praise Him for being worthy of your hope. Thank Him for His steadfast love.

PRAY INTO THE PSALM

Praying into Psalm 33

Add your own prayer points to the appropriate section(s) of A.C.T.S. (at right).

DRAW YOUR PRAYER POINTS FROM...

today's scripture: Psalm 33	your journal entries from today	today's additional thoughts for prayer

When ready, pray through your prayer points using the A.C.T.S. format.

Psalm 33 Prayer: A.C.T.S.

Adore God

Confess to God

Thank God

Ask God

DAY 10

Psalm 40

"Be still, and know that I am God"
– Psalm 46:10

■

Be settled physically
(but not too comfortable)

■

Ask the Holy Spirit to work in you
as you read God's Word

When ready, turn the page and read the entire psalm.

READ THE ENTIRE PSALM

Psalm 40

1 I waited patiently for the Lord;
he inclined to me and heard my cry.

2 He drew me up from the pit of destruction,
out of the miry bog, and set my feet
upon a rock, making my steps secure.

3 He put a new song in my mouth, a song of
praise to our God. Many will see and fear,
and put their trust in the Lord.

4 Blessed is the man who makes the Lord his
trust, who does not turn to the proud,
to those who go astray after a lie!

5 You have multiplied, O Lord my God,
your wondrous deeds and your thoughts
toward us; none can compare with you!
I will proclaim and tell of them,
yet they are more than can be told.

6 In sacrifice and offering you have
not delighted, but you have given me an
open ear. Burnt offering and sin offering
you have not required.

7 Then I said, "Behold, I have come;
in the scroll of the book it is written of me:

8 I delight to do your will, O my God;
your law is within my heart."

9 I have told the glad news of deliverance
in the great congregation;
behold, I have not restrained my lips,
as you know, O Lord.

10 I have not hidden your deliverance
within my heart; I have spoken of
your faithfulness and your salvation;
I have not concealed your steadfast love
and your faithfulness from the
great congregation.

11 As for you, O Lord, you will not restrain your
mercy from me; your steadfast love and your
faithfulness will ever preserve me!

12 For evils have encompassed me
beyond number; my iniquities have
overtaken me, and I cannot see;
they are more than the hairs of my head;
my heart fails me.

13 Be pleased, O Lord, to deliver me!
O Lord, make haste to help me!

14 Let those be put to shame and disappointed
altogether who seek to snatch away my life;
let those be turned back and brought
to dishonor who delight in my hurt!

15 Let those be appalled because of their shame
who say to me, "Aha, Aha!"

16 But may all who seek you rejoice and be glad
in you; may those who love your salvation
say continually, "Great is the Lord!"

17 As for me, I am poor and needy,
but the Lord takes thought for me.
You are my help and my deliverer;
do not delay, O my God!

MEDITATE ON THE PSALM

Think about what it says

Reflect on words or phrases that strike you

Circle or underline words or phrases that stand out

LET THE HOLY SPIRIT SPEAK TO YOU

When ready, begin journaling. Listen for and talk with God through your writing.

Psalm 40: My Observations

What thoughts came to your mind as you read the Word today?

Which word or phrase in the psalm struck you most significantly today?

WHAT HAPPENED?

What does this psalm say about who God is and what He has done?

What does this psalm say about who you are or what you should do?

Psalm 40: My Reflections

Reflect on the significance of the Word to you today.

Reflect on why you think the Spirit has drawn you to certain verses or details in this psalm.

SO WHAT?

How does this psalm connect with what is going on in your life *right now*?

Where does this psalm connect with patterns that you've seen *throughout your life*?

Psalm 40: My Response

Respond to
God through
your writing.

Write about
particular verses
or details the Spirit
is drawing your
attention toward.

NOW WHAT?

What can you
do *today*
in response
to God?

What changes in
your life do you feel
God is calling you
to make today?

When ready, turn the page and begin a time of prayer based on these observations, reflections and responses.

THOUGHTS FOR PRAYER

Notes

Psalm 40: Additional Thoughts for Prayer

Review some of the thoughts and emotions found in Psalm 40 and consider their related prayer points. Where applicable, note what the Holy Spirit brings to your attention (even if just one word).

Patience
Are you waiting patiently for God? Tell Him about it. If you are seriously struggling to be patient, cry out to Him and give Him your fear, anger, and/or pain. Ask Him to renew your strength, patience and trust.

Responsibility
Consider the phrase "hidden your deliverance within my heart" from verse 10. Does that apply to you? Who do you know that you can tell about God's steadfast love and faithfulness?

Deliverance
Adore God with the words from verse 16: "Great is the Lord!" Praise Him for being your deliverer.

PRAY INTO THE PSALM

Praying into Psalm 40

Add your own prayer points to the appropriate section(s) of A.C.T.S. (at right).

DRAW YOUR PRAYER POINTS FROM...

today's scripture: Psalm 40	your journal entries from today	today's additional thoughts for prayer

When ready, pray through your prayer points using the A.C.T.S. format.

Psalm 40 Prayer: A.C.T.S.

Adore God

Confess to God

Thank God

Ask God

DAY 11

Psalm 46

"Be still, and know that I am God"
– Psalm 46:10

■

Be settled physically
(but not too comfortable)

■

Ask the Holy Spirit to work in you
as you read God's Word

When ready, turn the page and read the entire psalm.

READ THE ENTIRE PSALM

Psalm 46

1 God is our refuge and strength,
a very present help in trouble.

2 Therefore we will not fear
though the earth gives way,
though the mountains be moved
into the heart of the sea,

3 though its waters roar and foam,
though the mountains tremble
at its swelling. *Selah*

4 There is a river whose streams make glad
the city of God, the holy habitation of the Most High.

5 God is in the midst of her; she shall not be moved;
God will help her when morning dawns.

6 The nations rage, the kingdoms totter;
he utters his voice, the earth melts.

7 The Lord of hosts is with us;
the God of Jacob is our fortress. *Selah*

8 Come, behold the works of the Lord,
how he has brought desolations on the earth.

9 He makes wars cease to the end of the earth;
he breaks the bow and shatters the spear;
he burns the chariots with fire.

10 "Be still, and know that I am God.
I will be exalted among the nations,
I will be exalted in the earth!"

11 The Lord of hosts is with us;
the God of Jacob is our fortress. *Selah*

MEDITATE ON THE PSALM

Think about what it says | Reflect on words or phrases that strike you | Circle or underline words or phrases that stand out

LET THE HOLY SPIRIT SPEAK TO YOU

When ready, begin journaling. Listen for and talk with God through your writing.

OBSERVATIONAL JOURNAL

Psalm 46: My Observations

What thoughts came to your mind as you read the Word today?

Which word or phrase in the psalm struck you most significantly today?

WHAT HAPPENED?

What does this psalm say about who God is and what He has done?

What does this psalm say about who you are or what you should do?

Psalm 46: My Reflections

Reflect on the significance of the Word to you today.

Reflect on why you think the Spirit has drawn you to certain verses or details in this psalm.

SO WHAT?

How does this psalm connect with what is going on in your life *right now*?

Where does this psalm connect with patterns that you've seen *throughout your life*?

Psalm 46: My Response

Respond to God through your writing.

Write about particular verses or details the Spirit is drawing your attention toward.

NOW WHAT?

What can you do *today* in response to God?

What changes in your life do you feel God is calling you to make today?

When ready, turn the page and begin a time of prayer based on these observations, reflections and responses.

THOUGHTS FOR PRAYER

Notes

Psalm 46: Additional Thoughts for Prayer

Review some of the thoughts and emotions found in Psalm 46 and consider their related prayer points. Where applicable, note what the Holy Spirit brings to your attention (even if just one word).

Refuge
What problems are you dealing with? Give them to Him.

Might
Do you ever attempt to rely on your own strength to handle life's challenges? Confess that to Him. Adore Him for His might.

Security
Ask God for His peace—to help you "be still." Tell Him about ways you are striving, trying to earn salvation. Give those to Him.

PRAY INTO THE PSALM

Praying into Psalm 46

Add your own prayer points to the appropriate section(s) of A.C.T.S. (at right).

DRAW YOUR PRAYER POINTS FROM...

today's scripture: Psalm 46	your journal entries from today	today's additional thoughts for prayer

When ready, pray through your prayer points using the A.C.T.S. format.

Psalm 46 Prayer: A.C.T.S.

Adore God

Confess to God

Thank God

Ask God

DAY 12

Psalm 49

"Be still, and know that I am God"
– Psalm 46:10

■

Be settled physically
(but not too comfortable)

■

Ask the Holy Spirit to work in you
as you read God's Word

When ready, turn the page and read the entire psalm.

READ THE ENTIRE PSALM

Psalm 49

1 Hear this, all peoples!
Give ear, all inhabitants of the world,
2 both low and high,
rich and poor together!
3 My mouth shall speak wisdom;
the meditation of my heart
shall be understanding.
4 I will incline my ear to a proverb;
I will solve my riddle to the music of the lyre.
5 Why should I fear in times of trouble,
when the iniquity of those who
cheat me surrounds me,
6 those who trust in their wealth and
boast of the abundance of their riches?
7 Truly no man can ransom another,
or give to God the price of his life,
8 for the ransom of their life is costly
and can never suffice,
9 that he should live on forever
and never see the pit.
10 For he sees that even the wise die;
the fool and the stupid alike must perish
and leave their wealth to others.
11 Their graves are their homes forever,
their dwelling places to all generations,
though they called lands
by their own names.
12 Man in his pomp will not remain;
he is like the beasts that perish.
13 This is the path of those who
have foolish confidence; yet after them
people approve of their boasts. *Selah*
14 Like sheep they are appointed for Sheol;
death shall be their shepherd, and the
upright shall rule over them in the morning.
Their form shall be consumed in Sheol,
with no place to dwell.
15 But God will ransom my soul from the power
of Sheol, for he will receive me. *Selah*
16 Be not afraid when a man becomes rich,
when the glory of his house increases.
17 For when he dies he will carry nothing away;
his glory will not go down after him.
18 For though, while he lives, he counts himself
blessed —and though you get praise when
you do well for yourself—
19 his soul will go to the generation of
his fathers, who will never again see light.
20 Man in his pomp yet without understanding
is like the beasts that perish.

MEDITATE ON THE PSALM

Think about what it says | Reflect on words or phrases that strike you | Circle or underline words or phrases that stand out

LET THE HOLY SPIRIT SPEAK TO YOU

When ready, begin journaling. Listen for and talk with God through your writing.

Psalm 49: My Observations

What thoughts came to your mind as you read the Word today?

Which word or phrase in the psalm struck you most significantly today?

WHAT HAPPENED?

What does this psalm say about who God is and what He has done?

What does this psalm say about who you are or what you should do?

Psalm 49: My Reflections

Reflect on the significance of the Word to you today.

Reflect on why you think the Spirit has drawn you to certain verses or details in this psalm.

SO WHAT?

How does this psalm connect with what is going on in your life *right now*?

Where does this psalm connect with patterns that you've seen *throughout your life*?

Psalm 49: My Response

Respond to God through your writing.

Write about particular verses or details the Spirit is drawing your attention toward.

NOW WHAT?

What can you do *today* in response to God?

What changes in your life do you feel God is calling you to make today?

When ready, turn the page and begin a time of prayer based on these observations, reflections and responses.

THOUGHTS FOR PRAYER

Notes

Psalm 49: Additional Thoughts for Prayer

Review some of the thoughts and emotions found in Psalm 49 and consider their related prayer points. Where applicable, note what the Holy Spirit brings to your attention (even if just one word).

Hearing
Thank God for speaking to you through His Word. Ask Him for help hearing it and applying its wisdom to your life.

Jesus
Do you struggle with admitting your need to be ransomed? Tell Him. Thank God for sending Jesus as the ransom for your soul.

Wisdom
What do you spend your time pursuing? If it is the world, tell God about it. Ask Him for more of His wisdom.

PRAY INTO THE PSALM

Praying into Psalm 49

Add your own prayer points to the appropriate section(s) of A.C.T.S. (at right).

DRAW YOUR PRAYER POINTS FROM...

today's scripture: Psalm 49	your journal entries from today	today's additional thoughts for prayer

When ready, pray through your prayer points using the A.C.T.S. format.

"Be still, and know that I am God"
– Psalm 46:10

■

Be settled physically
(but not too comfortable)

■

Ask the Holy Spirit to work in you
as you read God's Word

When ready, turn the page and read the entire psalm.

READ THE ENTIRE PSALM

Psalm 51

1 Have mercy on me, O God,
according to your steadfast love;
according to your abundant mercy
blot out my transgressions.

2 Wash me thoroughly from my iniquity,
and cleanse me from my sin!

3 For I know my transgressions,
and my sin is ever before me.

4 Against you, you only, have I sinned
and done what is evil in your sight,
so that you may be justified in your
words and blameless in your judgment.

5 Behold, I was brought forth in iniquity,
and in sin did my mother conceive me.

6 Behold, you delight in truth in
the inward being, and you teach me
wisdom in the secret heart.

7 Purge me with hyssop, and I shall be clean;
wash me, and I shall be whiter than snow.

8 Let me hear joy and gladness;
let the bones that you have broken rejoice.

9 Hide your face from my sins,
and blot out all my iniquities.

10 Create in me a clean heart, O God,
and renew a right spirit within me.

11 Cast me not away from your presence,
and take not your Holy Spirit from me.

12 Restore to me the joy of your salvation,
and uphold me with a willing spirit.

13 Then I will teach transgressors your ways,
and sinners will return to you.

14 Deliver me from bloodguiltiness, O God,
O God of my salvation, and my tongue will
sing aloud of your righteousness.

15 O Lord, open my lips,
and my mouth will declare your praise.

16 For you will not delight in sacrifice,
or I would give it; you will not be pleased
with a burnt offering.

17 The sacrifices of God are a broken spirit;
a broken and contrite heart, O God,
you will not despise.

18 Do good to Zion in your good pleasure;
build up the walls of Jerusalem;

19 then will you delight in right sacrifices,
in burnt offerings and whole burnt offerings;
then bulls will be offered on your altar.

MEDITATE ON THE PSALM

Think about what it says

Reflect on words or phrases that strike you

Circle or underline words or phrases that stand out

LET THE HOLY SPIRIT SPEAK TO YOU

When ready, begin journaling. Listen for and talk with God through your writing.

Psalm 51: My Observations

What thoughts came to your mind as you read the Word today?

Which word or phrase in the psalm struck you most significantly today?

WHAT HAPPENED?

What does this psalm say about who God is and what He has done?

What does this psalm say about who you are or what you should do?

Psalm 51: My Reflections

Reflect on the significance of the Word to you today.

Reflect on why you think the Spirit has drawn you to certain verses or details in this psalm.

SO WHAT?

How does this psalm connect with what is going on in your life *right now*?

Where does this psalm connect with patterns that you've seen *throughout your life*?

Psalm 51: My Response

Respond to God through your writing.

Write about particular verses or details the Spirit is drawing your attention toward.

NOW WHAT?

What can you do *today* in response to God?

What changes in your life do you feel God is calling you to make today?

When ready, turn the page and begin a time of prayer based on these observations, reflections and responses.

THOUGHTS FOR PRAYER

Notes

Psalm 51: Additional Thoughts for Prayer

Review some of the thoughts and emotions found in Psalm 51 and consider their related prayer points. Where applicable, note what the Holy Spirit brings to your attention (even if just one word).

Confession
Tell God about the "dirt" in your life. Praise Him for His mercy. Thank Him for His love.

Forgiveness
Think of being covered in dirt, sweat, and grime and how wonderful it feels to get cleaned up afterwards. Praise God for granting spiritual cleansing. Thank Him for His forgiveness.

Restoration
Ask Him for a renewed sense of His joy.

PRAY INTO THE PSALM

Praying into Psalm 51

Add your own prayer points to the appropriate section(s) of A.C.T.S. (at right).

DRAW YOUR PRAYER POINTS FROM...

today's scripture: Psalm 51	your journal entries from today	today's additional thoughts for prayer

When ready, pray through your prayer points using the A.C.T.S. format.

Psalm 51 Prayer: A.C.T.S.

Adore God

Confess to God

Thank God

Ask God

DAY 14

Psalm 73

"Be still, and know that I am God"
– Psalm 46:10

■

Be settled physically
(but not too comfortable)

■

Ask the Holy Spirit to work in you
as you read God's Word

When ready, turn the page and read the entire psalm.

READ THE ENTIRE PSALM

Psalm 73

1 Truly God is good to Israel,
to those who are pure in heart.

2 But as for me, my feet had almost stumbled,
my steps had nearly slipped.

3 For I was envious of the arrogant when
I saw the prosperity of the wicked.

4 For they have no pangs until death;
their bodies are fat and sleek.

5 They are not in trouble as others are;
they are not stricken like the rest of mankind.

6 Therefore pride is their necklace;
violence covers them as a garment.

7 Their eyes swell out through fatness;
their hearts overflow with follies.

8 They scoff and speak with malice;
loftily they threaten oppression.

9 They set their mouths against the heavens,
and their tongue struts through the earth.

10 Therefore his people turn back to them,
and find no fault in them.

11 And they say, "How can God know?
Is there knowledge in the Most High?"

12 Behold, these are the wicked;
always at ease, they increase in riches.

13 All in vain have I kept my heart clean
and washed my hands in innocence.

14 For all the day long I have been stricken
and rebuked every morning.

15 If I had said, "I will speak thus,"
I would have betrayed the generation
of your children.

16 But when I thought how to understand this,
it seemed to me a wearisome task,

17 until I went into the sanctuary of God;
then I discerned their end.

18 Truly you set them in slippery places;
you make them fall to ruin.

19 How they are destroyed in a moment,
swept away utterly by terrors!

20 Like a dream when one awakes,
O Lord, when you rouse yourself,
you despise them as phantoms.

21 When my soul was embittered,
when I was pricked in heart,

22 I was brutish and ignorant;
I was like a beast toward you.

23 Nevertheless, I am continually with you;
you hold my right hand.

24 You guide me with your counsel,
and afterward you will receive me to glory.

25 Whom have I in heaven but you?
And there is nothing on earth
that I desire besides you.

26 My flesh and my heart may fail,
but God is the strength of my heart
and my portion forever.

27 For behold, those who are far from
you shall perish; you put an end to
everyone who is unfaithful to you.

28 But for me it is good to be near God;
I have made the Lord God my refuge,
that I may tell of all your works.

MEDITATE ON THE PSALM

Think about what it says

Reflect on words or phrases that strike you

Circle or underline words or phrases that stand out

LET THE HOLY SPIRIT SPEAK TO YOU

When ready, begin journaling. Listen for and talk with God through your writing.

Psalm 73: My Observations

What thoughts came to your mind as you read the Word today?

Which word or phrase in the psalm struck you most significantly today?

WHAT HAPPENED?

What does this psalm say about who God is and what He has done?

What does this psalm say about who you are or what you should do?

Psalm 73: My Reflections

Reflect on the significance of the Word to you today.

Reflect on why you think the Spirit has drawn you to certain verses or details in this psalm.

SO WHAT?

How does this psalm connect with what is going on in your life *right now*?

Where does this psalm connect with patterns that you've seen *throughout your life*?

Psalm 73: My Response

Respond to
God through
your writing.

Write about
particular verses
or details the Spirit
is drawing your
attention toward.

NOW WHAT?

What can you
do *today*
in response
to God?

What changes in
your life do you feel
God is calling you
to make today?

When ready, turn the page and begin a time of prayer based on these observations, reflections and responses.

THOUGHTS FOR PRAYER

Notes

Psalm 73: Additional Thoughts for Prayer

Review some of the thoughts and emotions found in Psalm 73 and consider their related prayer points. Where applicable, note what the Holy Spirit brings to your attention (even if just one word).

Wisdom
Consider the phrase "pride is their necklace."
Does that apply to you today? Give it to God.
Ask Him for His wisdom today.

Guidance
Give God the challenges you're facing. Ask Him for guidance. Thank Him for holding your right hand when you stumble.

Refuge
Thank God for being a refuge. Ask Him to be near you.

PRAY INTO THE PSALM

Praying into Psalm 73

Add your own prayer points to the appropriate section(s) of A.C.T.S. (at right).

DRAW YOUR PRAYER POINTS FROM...

today's scripture: Psalm 73	your journal entries from today	today's additional thoughts for prayer

When ready, pray through your prayer points using the A.C.T.S. format.

Psalm 73 Prayer: A.C.T.S.

Adore God

Confess to God

Thank God

Ask God

DAY
15

Psalm 86

"Be still, and know that I am God"
– Psalm 46:10

■

Be settled physically
(but not too comfortable)

■

Ask the Holy Spirit to work in you
as you read God's Word

When ready, turn the page and read the entire psalm.

READ THE ENTIRE PSALM

Psalm 86

1 Incline your ear, O Lord, and answer me,
for I am poor and needy.

2 Preserve my life, for I am godly;
save your servant, who trusts in
you—you are my God.

3 Be gracious to me, O Lord,
for to you do I cry all the day.

4 Gladden the soul of your servant,
for to you, O Lord, do I lift up my soul.

5 For you, O Lord, are good and forgiving,
abounding in steadfast love
to all who call upon you.

6 Give ear, O Lord, to my prayer;
listen to my plea for grace.

7 In the day of my trouble I call upon you,
for you answer me.

8 There is none like you among the gods,
O Lord, nor are there any works like yours.

9 All the nations you have made shall come
and worship before you, O Lord,
and shall glorify your name.

10 For you are great and do wondrous things;
you alone are God.

11 Teach me your way, O Lord,
that I may walk in your truth;
unite my heart to fear your name.

12 I give thanks to you, O Lord my God,
with my whole heart,
and I will glorify your name forever.

13 For great is your steadfast love toward me;
you have delivered my soul
from the depths of Sheol.

14 O God, insolent men have risen up against
me; a band of ruthless men seeks my life,
and they do not set you before them.

15 But you, O Lord, are a God merciful and
gracious, slow to anger and abounding in
steadfast love and faithfulness.

16 Turn to me and be gracious to me; give your
strength to your servant, and save the son
of your maidservant.

17 Show me a sign of your favor, that those
who hate me may see and be put to
shame because you, Lord, have helped
me and comforted me.

MEDITATE ON THE PSALM

Think about what it says

Reflect on words or phrases that strike you

Circle or underline words or phrases that stand out

LET THE HOLY SPIRIT SPEAK TO YOU

When ready, begin journaling. Listen for and talk with God through your writing.

Psalm 86: My Observations

What thoughts came to your mind as you read the Word today?

Which word or phrase in the psalm struck you most significantly today?

WHAT HAPPENED?

What does this psalm say about who God is and what He has done?

What does this psalm say about who you are or what you should do?

Psalm 86: My Reflections

Reflect on the significance of the Word to you today.

Reflect on why you think the Spirit has drawn you to certain verses or details in this psalm.

SO WHAT?

How does this psalm connect with what is going on in your life *right now*?

Where does this psalm connect with patterns that you've seen *throughout your life*?

Psalm 86: My Response

Respond to God through your writing.

Write about particular verses or details the Spirit is drawing your attention toward.

NOW WHAT?

What can you do *today* in response to God?

What changes in your life do you feel God is calling you to make today?

When ready, turn the page and begin a time of prayer based on these observations, reflections and responses.

THOUGHTS FOR PRAYER

Notes

Psalm 86: Additional Thoughts for Prayer

Review some of the thoughts and emotions found in Psalm 86 and consider their related prayer points. Where applicable, note what the Holy Spirit brings to your attention (even if just one word).

Lament
Do you feel like God doesn't hear you? Tell Him. Ask Him for a greater measure of His love.

Thankfulness
Is there a part of your heart that feels unable to thank to God today? Give that to Him. Ask Him to unite your heart. Thank Him with your whole heart using the words from verse 13: "You have delivered my soul from the depths of Sheol."

Faithfulness
Think of examples of God's faithfulness in your life. Thank Him for the specific examples that come to mind. Praise Him for His faithfulness.

PRAY INTO THE PSALM

Praying into Psalm 86

Add your own prayer points to the appropriate section(s) of A.C.T.S. (at right).

DRAW YOUR PRAYER POINTS FROM...

today's scripture: Psalm 86	your journal entries from today	today's additional thoughts for prayer

When ready, pray through your prayer points using the A.C.T.S. format.

Psalm 86 Prayer: A.C.T.S.

Adore God

Confess to God

Thank God

Ask God

DAY 16

Psalm 90

"Be still, and know that I am God"
– Psalm 46:10

Be settled physically
(but not too comfortable)

Ask the Holy Spirit to work in you
as you read God's Word

When ready, turn the page and read the entire psalm.

READ THE ENTIRE PSALM

Psalm 90

1 Lord, you have been our dwelling place
in all generations.

2 Before the mountains were brought forth,
or ever you had formed the earth
and the world, from everlasting
to everlasting you are God.

3 You return man to dust and say,
"Return, O children of man!"

4 For a thousand years in your sight
are but as yesterday when it is past,
or as a watch in the night.

5 You sweep them away as with a flood;
they are like a dream, like grass that is
renewed in the morning:

6 in the morning it flourishes and is renewed;
in the evening it fades and withers.

7 For we are brought to an end by your anger;
by your wrath we are dismayed.

8 You have set our iniquities before you,
our secret sins in the light of your presence.

9 For all our days pass away under your wrath;
we bring our years to an end like a sigh.

10 The years of our life are seventy,
or even by reason of strength eighty;
yet their span is but toil and trouble;
they are soon gone, and we fly away.

11 Who considers the power of your anger,
and your wrath according to the fear of you?

12 So teach us to number our days
that we may get a heart of wisdom.

13 Return, O Lord! How long?
Have pity on your servants!

14 Satisfy us in the morning with your
steadfast love, that we may rejoice
and be glad all our days.

15 Make us glad for as many days as you
have afflicted us, and for as many
years as we have seen evil.

16 Let your work be shown to your servants,
and your glorious power to their children.

17 Let the favor of the Lord our God be upon us,
and establish the work of our hands upon
us; yes, establish the work of our hands!

MEDITATE ON THE PSALM

Think about what it says

Reflect on words or phrases that strike you

Circle or underline words or phrases that stand out

LET THE HOLY SPIRIT SPEAK TO YOU

When ready, begin journaling. Listen for and talk with God through your writing.

Psalm 90: My Observations

What thoughts came to your mind as you read the Word today?

Which word or phrase in the psalm struck you most significantly today?

WHAT HAPPENED?

What does this psalm say about who God is and what He has done?

What does this psalm say about who you are or what you should do?

Psalm 90: My Reflections

Reflect on the significance of the Word to you today.

Reflect on why you think the Spirit has drawn you to certain verses or details in this psalm.

SO WHAT?

How does this psalm connect with what is going on in your life *right now*?

Where does this psalm connect with patterns that you've seen *throughout your life*?

Psalm 90: My Response

Respond to God through your writing.

Write about particular verses or details the Spirit is drawing your attention toward.

NOW WHAT?

What can you do *today* in response to God?

What changes in your life do you feel God is calling you to make today?

When ready, turn the page and begin a time of prayer based on these observations, reflections and responses.

THOUGHTS FOR PRAYER

Notes

Psalm 90: Additional Thoughts for Prayer

Review some of the thoughts and emotions found in Psalm 90 and consider their related prayer points. Where applicable, note what the Holy Spirit brings to your attention (even if just one word).

Home
Praise God for His presence. Thank HIm for the comfort and security He provides.

Understanding
Ask Him to teach you to number your days.
Thank Him for the understanding He provides.
Ask Him for a daily dose of His unfailing love.

Provision
Thank Him for the favor of His provision. Ask Him to bless your work.

PRAY INTO THE PSALM

Praying into Psalm 90

Add your own prayer points to the appropriate section(s) of A.C.T.S. (at right).

DRAW YOUR PRAYER POINTS FROM...

today's scripture: Psalm 90

your journal entries from today

today's additional thoughts for prayer

When ready, pray through your prayer points using the A.C.T.S. format.

Psalm 90 Prayer: A.C.T.S.

Adore God

Confess to God

Thank God

Ask God

DAY 17

Psalm 100

"Be still, and know that I am God"
– Psalm 46:10

■

Be settled physically
(but not too comfortable)

■

Ask the Holy Spirit to work in you
as you read God's Word

When ready, turn the page and read the entire psalm.

READ THE ENTIRE PSALM

Psalm 100

1 Make a joyful noise to the Lord, all the earth!
2 Serve the Lord with gladness!
Come into his presence with singing!
3 Know that the Lord, he is God!
It is he who made us, and we are his;
we are his people, and the sheep of his pasture.
4 Enter his gates with thanksgiving,
and his courts with praise!
Give thanks to him; bless his name!
5 For the Lord is good;
his steadfast love endures forever,
and his faithfulness to all generations.

MEDITATE ON THE PSALM

Think about what it says | Reflect on words or phrases that strike you | Circle or underline words or phrases that stand out

LET THE HOLY SPIRIT SPEAK TO YOU

When ready, begin journaling. Listen for and talk with God through your writing.

Psalm 100: My Observations

What thoughts came to your mind as you read the Word today?

Which word or phrase in the psalm struck you most significantly today?

WHAT HAPPENED?

What does this psalm say about who God is and what He has done?

What does this psalm say about who you are or what you should do?

Psalm 100: My Reflections

Reflect on the significance of the Word to you today.

Reflect on why you think the Spirit has drawn you to certain verses or details in this psalm.

SO WHAT?

How does this psalm connect with what is going on in your life *right now*?

Where does this psalm connect with patterns that you've seen *throughout your life*?

Psalm 100: My Response

Respond to God through your writing.

Write about particular verses or details the Spirit is drawing your attention toward.

NOW WHAT?

What can you do *today* in response to God?

What changes in your life do you feel God is calling you to make today?

When ready, turn the page and begin a time of prayer based on these observations, reflections and responses.

THOUGHTS FOR PRAYER

Notes

Psalm 100: Additional Thoughts for Prayer

Review some of the thoughts and emotions found in Psalm 100 and consider their related prayer points. Where applicable, note what the Holy Spirit brings to your attention (even if just one word).

Serving
How do you serve God? In what ways do you show your thankfulness for His grace?

Belonging
Adore Him as your creator. Praise Him for the security you have in belonging to Him.

Thanksgiving
Thank and praise Him for the specific ways He shows His faithfulness to you.

PRAY INTO THE PSALM

Praying into Psalm 100

Add your own prayer points to the appropriate section(s) of A.C.T.S. (at right).

DRAW YOUR PRAYER POINTS FROM...

today's scripture: Psalm 100	your journal entries from today	today's additional thoughts for prayer

When ready, pray through your prayer points using the A.C.T.S. format.

Psalm 100 Prayer: A.C.T.S.

Adore God

Confess to God

Thank God

Ask God

DAY 18

Psalm 103

"Be still, and know that I am God"
– Psalm 46:10

■

Be settled physically
(but not too comfortable)

■

Ask the Holy Spirit to work in you
as you read God's Word

When ready, turn the page and read the entire psalm.

READ THE ENTIRE PSALM

Psalm 103

1 Bless the Lord, O my soul,
and all that is within me,
bless his holy name!

2 Bless the Lord, O my soul,
and forget not all his benefits,

3 who forgives all your iniquity,
who heals all your diseases,

4 who redeems your life from the pit,
who crowns you with steadfast
love and mercy,

5 who satisfies you with good
so that your youth is renewed
like the eagle's.

6 The Lord works righteousness
and justice for all who are oppressed.

7 He made known his ways to Moses,
his acts to the people of Israel.

8 The Lord is merciful and gracious,
slow to anger and abounding
in steadfast love.

9 He will not always chide,
nor will he keep his anger forever.

10 He does not deal with us
according to our sins, nor repay us
according to our iniquities.

11 For as high as the heavens are
above the earth, so great is his steadfast
love toward those who fear him;

12 as far as the east is from the west,
so far does he remove our
transgressions from us.

13 As a father shows compassion to
his children, so the Lord shows compassion
to those who fear him.

14 For he knows our frame;
he remembers that we are dust.

15 As for man, his days are like grass;
he flourishes like a flower of the field;

16 for the wind passes over it, and it is gone,
and its place knows it no more.

17 But the steadfast love of the Lord
is from everlasting to everlasting
on those who fear him, and his
righteousness to children's children,

18 to those who keep his covenant
and remember to do his commandments.

19 The Lord has established his throne
in the heavens, and his kingdom
rules over all.

20 Bless the Lord, O you his angels,
you mighty ones who do his word,
obeying the voice of his word!

21 Bless the Lord, all his hosts,
his ministers, who do his will!

22 Bless the Lord, all his works,
in all places of his dominion.
Bless the Lord, O my soul!.

MEDITATE ON THE PSALM

Think about what it says

Reflect on words or phrases that strike you

Circle or underline words or phrases that stand out

LET THE HOLY SPIRIT SPEAK TO YOU

When ready, begin journaling. Listen for and talk with God through your writing.

Psalm 103: My Observations

What thoughts came to your mind as you read the Word today?

Which word or phrase in the psalm struck you most significantly today?

WHAT HAPPENED?

What does this psalm say about who God is and what He has done?

What does this psalm say about who you are or what you should do?

Psalm 103: My Reflections

Reflect on the significance of the Word to you today.

Reflect on why you think the Spirit has drawn you to certain verses or details in this psalm.

SO WHAT?

How does this psalm connect with what is going on in your life *right now*?

Where does this psalm connect with patterns that you've seen *throughout your life*?

Psalm 103: My Response

Respond to God through your writing.

Write about particular verses or details the Spirit is drawing your attention toward.

NOW WHAT?

What can you do *today* in response to God?

What changes in your life do you feel God is calling you to make today?

When ready, turn the page and begin a time of prayer based on these observations, reflections and responses.

THOUGHTS FOR PRAYER

Notes

Psalm 103: Additional Thoughts for Prayer

Review some of the thoughts and emotions found in Psalm 103 and consider their related prayer points. Where applicable, note what the Holy Spirit brings to your attention (even if just one word).

Praise
Meditate on verse 1: "Bless the Lord, O my soul, and all that is within me, bless his holy name!" Is that easy for you to do today, or difficult? Either way, note why you feel the way you do.

Mercy
Are you struggling with any bad habits? Give them to Him. Thank God for His mercy and grace. Ask Him for strength to overcome temptation.

Steadfastness
Thank God for the people in your life who have reflected God's love to you. How can you reflect God's steadfast love to the people He has brought into your life?

PRAY INTO THE PSALM

Praying into Psalm 103

Add your own prayer points to the appropriate section(s) of A.C.T.S. (at right).

DRAW YOUR PRAYER POINTS FROM...

today's scripture: Psalm 103	your journal entries from today	today's additional thoughts for prayer

When ready, pray through your prayer points using the A.C.T.S. format.

Psalm 103 Prayer: A.C.T.S.

Adore God

Confess to God

Thank God

Ask God

DAY
19

Psalm 121

"Be still, and know that I am God"
– Psalm 46:10

■

Be settled physically
(but not too comfortable)

■

Ask the Holy Spirit to work in you
as you read God's Word

When ready, turn the page and read the entire psalm.

READ THE ENTIRE PSALM

Psalm 121

1 I lift up my eyes to the hills.
From where does my help come?

2 My help comes from the Lord,
who made heaven and earth.

3 He will not let your foot be moved;
he who keeps you will not slumber.

4 Behold, he who keeps Israel
will neither slumber nor sleep.

5 The Lord is your keeper;
the Lord is your shade on your right hand.

6 The sun shall not strike you by day,
nor the moon by night.

7 The Lord will keep you from all evil;
he will keep your life.

8 The Lord will keep your going out
and your coming in from this time
forth and forevermore.

MEDITATE ON THE PSALM

Think about what it says

Reflect on words or phrases that strike you

Circle or underline words or phrases that stand out

LET THE HOLY SPIRIT SPEAK TO YOU

When ready, begin journaling. Listen for and talk with God through your writing.

Psalm 121: My Observations

What thoughts came to your mind as you read the Word today?

Which word or phrase in the psalm struck you most significantly today?

WHAT HAPPENED?

What does this psalm say about who God is and what He has done?

What does this psalm say about who you are or what you should do?

Psalm 121: My Reflections

Reflect on the significance of the Word to you today.

Reflect on why you think the Spirit has drawn you to certain verses or details in this psalm.

SO WHAT?

How does this psalm connect with what is going on in your life *right now*?

Where does this psalm connect with patterns that you've seen *throughout your life*?

Psalm 121: My Response

Respond to
God through
your writing.

Write about
particular verses
or details the Spirit
is drawing your
attention toward.

**NOW
WHAT?**

What can you
do *today*
in response
to God?

What changes in
your life do you feel
God is calling you
to make today?

When ready, turn the page and begin a time of prayer based on these observations, reflections and responses.

THOUGHTS FOR PRAYER

Notes

Psalm 121: Additional Thoughts for Prayer

Review some of the thoughts and emotions found in Psalm 121 and consider their related prayer points. Where applicable, note what the Holy Spirit brings to your attention (even if just one word).

Encouragement
Adore God for His might. Take encouragement from His unchanging nature.

Hope
Thank God for being ever-present. Tell Him about the things that erode your hope and give them to Him. Thank Him for His promise to watch over you.

Peace
Adore God for being eternal. Ask Him for a greater measure of His peace.

PRAY INTO THE PSALM

Praying into Psalm 121

Add your own prayer points to the appropriate section(s) of A.C.T.S. (at right).

DRAW YOUR PRAYER POINTS FROM...

today's scripture: Psalm 121	your journal entries from today	today's additional thoughts for prayer

When ready, pray through your prayer points using the A.C.T.S. format.

Psalm 121 Prayer: A.C.T.S.

Adore God

Confess to God

Thank God

Ask God

DAY 20

Psalm 136

"Be still, and know that I am God"
– Psalm 46:10

■

Be settled physically
(but not too comfortable)

■

Ask the Holy Spirit to work in you
as you read God's Word

When ready, turn the page and read the entire psalm.

READ THE ENTIRE PSALM

Psalm 136

1 Give thanks to the Lord, for he is good,
for his steadfast love endures forever.

2 Give thanks to the God of gods,
for his steadfast love endures forever.

3 Give thanks to the Lord of lords,
for his steadfast love endures forever;

4 to him who alone does great wonders,
for his steadfast love endures forever;

5 to him who by understanding made
the heavens, for his steadfast
love endures forever;

6 to him who spread out the earth above
the waters, for his steadfast
love endures forever;

7 to him who made the great lights,
for his steadfast love endures forever;

8 the sun to rule over the day,
for his steadfast love endures forever;

9 the moon and stars to rule over the night,
for his steadfast love endures forever;

10 to him who struck down the firstborn of Egypt,
for his steadfast love endures forever;

11 and brought Israel out from among them,
for his steadfast love endures forever;

12 with a strong hand and an outstretched arm,
for his steadfast love endures forever;

13 to him who divided the Red Sea in two,
for his steadfast love endures forever;

14 and made Israel pass through the midst of it,
for his steadfast love endures forever;

15 but overthrew Pharaoh and his host in
the Red Sea, for his steadfast
love endures forever;

16 to him who led his people through
the wilderness, for his steadfast
love endures forever;

17 to him who struck down great kings,
for his steadfast love endures forever;

18 and killed mighty kings,
for his steadfast love endures forever;

19 Sihon, king of the Amorites,
for his steadfast love endures forever;

20 and Og, king of Bashan,
for his steadfast love endures forever;

21 and gave their land as a heritage,
for his steadfast love endures forever;

22 a heritage to Israel his servant,
for his steadfast love endures forever.

23 It is he who remembered us in our low estate,
for his steadfast love endures forever;

24 and rescued us from our foes,
for his steadfast love endures forever;

25 he who gives food to all flesh,
for his steadfast love endures forever.

26 Give thanks to the God of heaven,
for his steadfast love endures forever.

MEDITATE ON THE PSALM

Think about what it says

Reflect on words or phrases that strike you

Circle or underline words or phrases that stand out

LET THE HOLY SPIRIT SPEAK TO YOU

When ready, begin journaling. Listen for and talk with God through your writing.

Psalm 136: My Observations

What thoughts came to your mind as you read the Word today?

Which word or phrase in the psalm struck you most significantly today?

WHAT HAPPENED?

What does this psalm say about who God is and what He has done?

What does this psalm say about who you are or what you should do?

REFLECTIVE
JOURNAL

Psalm 136: My Reflections

Reflect on the significance of the Word to you today.

Reflect on why you think the Spirit has drawn you to certain verses or details in this psalm.

SO WHAT?

How does this psalm connect with what is going on in your life *right now*?

Where does this psalm connect with patterns that you've seen *throughout your life*?

Psalm 136: My Response

Respond to God through your writing.

Write about particular verses or details the Spirit is drawing your attention toward.

NOW WHAT?

What can you do *today* in response to God?

What changes in your life do you feel God is calling you to make today?

When ready, turn the page and begin a time of prayer based on these observations, reflections and responses.

THOUGHTS FOR PRAYER

Notes

Psalm 136: Additional Thoughts for Prayer

Review some of the thoughts and emotions found in Psalm 136 and consider their related prayer points. Where applicable, note what the Holy Spirit brings to your attention (even if just one word).

Thankfulness
What you are thankful for today? Note some of the things that come to mind, and thank God for them. Adore Him for His wonders.

Steadfast Love
Ask God for His steadfast love today using Psalm 90:14: "Satisfy us in the morning with your steadfast love, that we may rejoice and be glad all our days."

Goodness
Adore Him for being a good, good Father.
Thank Him for not basing His love upon your performance or significance.

PRAY INTO THE PSALM

Praying into Psalm 136

Add your own prayer points to the appropriate section(s) of A.C.T.S. (at right).

DRAW YOUR PRAYER POINTS FROM...

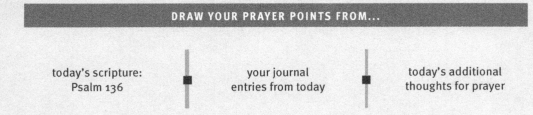

today's scripture: Psalm 136	your journal entries from today	today's additional thoughts for prayer

When ready, pray through your prayer points using the A.C.T.S. format.

PRAY

Psalm 136 Prayer: A.C.T.S.

Adore God

Confess to God

Thank God

Ask God

DAY 21

Psalm 139

"Be still, and know that I am God"
– *Psalm 46:10*

Be settled physically
(but not too comfortable)

Ask the Holy Spirit to work in you
as you read God's Word

When ready, turn the page and read the entire psalm.

READ THE ENTIRE PSALM

Psalm 139

1 O Lord, you have searched me
and known me!

2 You know when I sit down and when I rise up;
you discern my thoughts from afar.

3 You search out my path and my lying down
and are acquainted with all my ways.

4 Even before a word is on my tongue,
behold, O Lord, you know it altogether.

5 You hem me in, behind and before,
and lay your hand upon me.

6 Such knowledge is too wonderful for me;
it is high; I cannot attain it.

7 Where shall I go from your Spirit?
Or where shall I flee from your presence?

8 If I ascend to heaven, you are there!
If I make my bed in Sheol, you are there!

9 If I take the wings of the morning and
dwell in the uttermost parts of the sea,

10 even there your hand shall lead me,
and your right hand shall hold me.

11 If I say, "Surely the darkness shall cover me,
and the light about me be night,"

12 even the darkness is not dark to you;
the night is bright as the day,
for darkness is as light with you.

13 For you formed my inward parts;
you knitted me together
in my mother's womb.

14 I praise you, for I am fearfully
and wonderfully made.
Wonderful are your works;
my soul knows it very well.

15 My frame was not hidden from you,
when I was being made in secret,
intricately woven in the depths of the earth.

16 Your eyes saw my unformed substance;
in your book were written, every one of
them, the days that were formed for me,
when as yet there was none of them.

17 How precious to me are your thoughts, O God!
How vast is the sum of them!

18 If I would count them, they are more than the
sand. I awake, and I am still with you.

19 Oh that you would slay the wicked, O God!
O men of blood, depart from me!

20 They speak against you with malicious intent;
your enemies take your name in vain.

21 Do I not hate those who hate you, O Lord?
And do I not loathe those who rise up
against you?

22 I hate them with complete hatred;
I count them my enemies.

23 Search me, O God, and know my heart!
Try me and know my thoughts!

24 And see if there be any grievous way in me,
and lead me in the way everlasting!

MEDITATE ON THE PSALM

Think about what it says

Reflect on words or phrases that strike you

Circle or underline words or phrases that stand out

LET THE HOLY SPIRIT SPEAK TO YOU

When ready, begin journaling. Listen for and talk with God through your writing.

Psalm 139: My Observations

What thoughts came to your mind as you read the Word today?

Which word or phrase in the psalm struck you most significantly today?

WHAT HAPPENED?

What does this psalm say about who God is and what He has done?

What does this psalm say about who you are or what you should do?

Psalm 139: My Reflections

Reflect on the significance of the Word to you today.

Reflect on why you think the Spirit has drawn you to certain verses or details in this psalm.

SO WHAT?

How does this psalm connect with what is going on in your life *right now*?

Where does this psalm connect with patterns that you've seen *throughout your life*?

Psalm 139: My Response

Respond to God through your writing.

Write about particular verses or details the Spirit is drawing your attention toward.

NOW WHAT?

What can you do *today* in response to God?

What changes in your life do you feel God is calling you to make today?

When ready, turn the page and begin a time of prayer based on these observations, reflections and responses.

THOUGHTS FOR PRAYER

Notes

Psalm 139: Additional Thoughts for Prayer

Review some of the thoughts and emotions found in Psalm 139 and consider their related prayer points. Where applicable, note what the Holy Spirit brings to your attention (even if just one word).

Praise
Praise God for having complete knowledge of your life. Adore His omniscience. Thank Him for caring for you and knowing you.

Wonder
What comes to mind when you consider God's wonderful works? Praise Him for them. Thank Him for how He intricately made you.

Precious
Adore Him for His thoughts. Thank Him for His precious Word. Ask Him to continue to reveal Himself to you as you study it.

PRAY INTO THE PSALM

Praying into Psalm 139

Add your own prayer points to the appropriate section(s) of A.C.T.S. (at right).

DRAW YOUR PRAYER POINTS FROM...

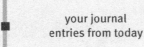

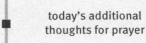

today's scripture: Psalm 139	your journal entries from today	today's additional thoughts for prayer

When ready, pray through your prayer points using the A.C.T.S. format.

Psalm 139 Prayer: A.C.T.S.

Adore God

Confess to God

Thank God

Ask God

Would you consider leaving a review of *Psalms Journal*?

Your review might help other readers discover *Psalms Journal*, so please consider leaving an honest review on Goodreads, Amazon or your favorite review site. It's the easiest way you can support our efforts.

Made in the USA
Monee, IL
15 May 2023

33721433R00103